GW01071828

Zoo feeding™

Auckland Zoo & Jon Gadsby

RANDOM HOUSE
NEW ZEALAND

GIRAFFE

If I really stretch my tongue
And stretch
And stretch
And nearly . . .
Yummy
Juicy leaves to munch and crunch
Then down my neck
To fill my tummy

See, when it comes to animals
The tallest of them, I'm among
But if you think my neck is long
Just wait until you see my tongue

My tongue can reach my tea with ease
So yes,
I'll have another please

DID YOU KNOW?

- There are four giraffes in Giraffe Valley at Auckland Zoo — Kay (in the picture), Zabulu, Rukiya and Ndale.
- Giraffes eat the leaves and buds from bushes and trees. They can spend 16–20 hours a day feeding. No wonder they often sleep standing up!
- Besides leaves from branches, the Zoo's giraffes are fed hay, pellets, fruit and vegetables.
- Their tongues are up to 46cm long and are black on the end. It is thought that this protects the tongues from sunburn.

WHITE RHINOCEROS

Hey watch my hand!
Hey watch my hay
I've waited for my hay all day

I've rolled in mud
And got all wet
And now I'm hungry you can bet

Now I can smell
And sort of tell
Not far away — delicious hay
Mmmm

I'll move in close
Don't want to waste it
There it is
And now — to taste it

Hey mind my hand!
Hey mind my hay
I wish that hand would go away

DID YOU KNOW?

- This is Mandhla, a male white rhinoceros.
- In the wild, white rhinos graze on grass which they crop using their lips, not their teeth.
- Why is the rhinoceros called 'white' when it is grey in colour? Its name actually comes from the Afrikaans word 'weit', meaning 'wide' — 'wide-mouthed' rhinoceros.
- A rhino's horn is made of thousands of strands of very stiff hair!

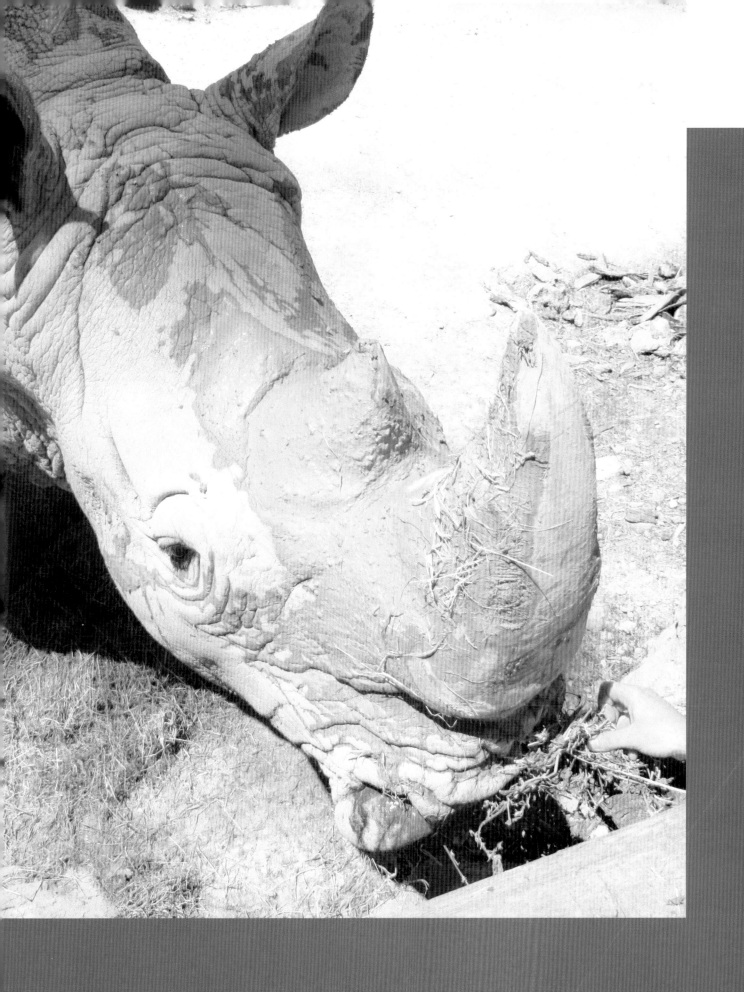

ORIENTAL SMALL-CLAWED OTTER

Fish is tasty, fish is fine
Fish is scrumptious, fish is mine

Fishy flavour, finny crunch
Perfect for an otter lunch

In the water, otter master
Fish is fast but otter faster

Fish is darting, fish is racing
Otter diving, otter chasing

Fish is swerving, otter matches
Fish is cornered, otter catches

On the bank for otter lunch
Finny flavour, fishy crunch

DID YOU KNOW?

- This is Jade, an Oriental small-clawed otter.
- Otters are carnivores. They feed on fish, eels and shellfish in rivers.
- At the Auckland Zoo, the keepers often hide the otters' food in floating logs, and sometimes place live eels into the enclosure so the otters can perfect their hunting skills.
- In the water otters seem to take on a silver sheen. This is caused by a film of air bubbles, which clings to their coats.

BORNEAN ORANG-UTAN

Boring bananas again
It's really becoming a pain
I'd like to be thinner
But breakfast and dinner
Is boring bananas again

Why can't they give me some toast?
Spaghetti, baked beans or a roast
I'd love a nice muffin
But no, I get nuffin'
But boring bananas again

But — this one's not bad
Over-ripe, just a tad
So might as well swallow it
Then maybe follow it . . .

With . . .
Boring bananas again
Another banana, I feel it
At least I remembered to peel it

DID YOU KNOW?

- This is Indra, a female Bornean orang-utan. Indra's big belly isn't due to pregnancy — it's just a sign of her age and that she enjoys her food!
- Auckland Zoo has a large group of Bornean orang-utans with males Horst, Charlie and Isim, and females Indra, Intan, Gansa, Metur and Wanita.
- Orang-utans eat mainly fruit, leaves, shoots, insects and tree bark, and the occasional egg.
- Bornean orang-utans are very intelligent and often find food by watching where other fruit-eating animals are feeding.

HIPPOPOTAMUS

When you're as big as me
You need a lot of tea
I'd soon become much thinner
If I didn't eat my dinner
So watch me as I munch and crunch
My hefty hippo-helping lunch
Perhaps I'll have a rest at length
But meantime, well, I need my strength

I think I need more hay indeed
More hay at once, I think I need
Now honestly, it isn't greed
Us hippos take a lot to feed

DID YOU KNOW?

- Auckland Zoo's three hippos, Faith, Fudge and Snorkel, are fed bales of hay (like Faith in the picture) as well as lettuce, carrots, pellets and vitamin supplements.
- Hippopotamus means 'river horse'. Hippos adore wallowing in water and spend most of their time in it.
- On land hippos are not at all slow — they can easily outrun a human.
- Hippos have pink sweat. It acts like sunscreen, and helps any wounds or infections in their skin to heal.

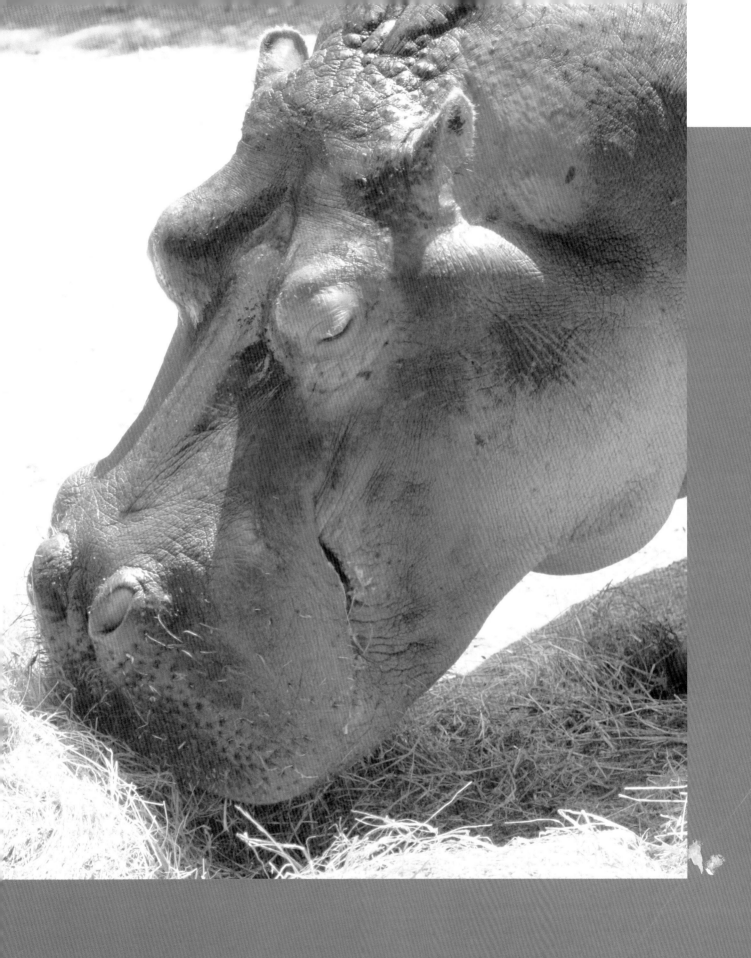

LITTLE BLUE PENGUIN

Little blue penguins wait for fish
Hope you've got some fish, they wish
Little blue penguins form a queue
Line up, here's some fish for you

Sprats and smelt and shrimps and dory
Baitfish, great fish, that's the story
Fine fish, fresh fish — just can't match it
Better still, no need to catch it

Little blue penguins, flip, flap, flop
Feeding time so up they hop
Little blue penguins wait in line
Dinner's here and that's just fine

DID YOU KNOW?

- Stella is being fed by Zoo Team Leader Andrew Nelson. There are five little blue penguins at Auckland Zoo.
- Of the 17 species of penguin worldwide, the blue penguin is the littlest.
- The main food of the little blue penguin is fish, and they also like squid and crustaceans. They swim out to a good place and dive for their catch, holding their breath underwater for up to two minutes!
- Penguins feed their chicks by storing fish in their stomachs and regurgitating it.

GALÁPAGOS TORTOISES

What you eating, tortoise?
What you get today?
What you munching tortoise
In your crunchy tortoise way?

I'm dining on some tender stalks
Of munchy-crunch bamboo
And then I'll have a nibble on
Some grass, before I'm through

Us tortoises are herbivores
So plants are what we eat
And cactus is our favourite
Oh prickles! What a treat

Cactus tickles
Juicy trickles
All those prickles
What a treat

Cactus is a tortoise winner
'Scuse me while I have my dinner

DID YOU KNOW?

- Munching on banana palm, from left, are Snapper, Smiley, and Willie.
- The Auckland Zoo has four of these magnificent tortoises, which come only from the Galápagos Islands. They can live for at least 150 years and so the Zoo's four, in their 30s, are just youngsters.
- Galápagos tortoises are herbivores. They like to graze on grass — especially young grass — and other plants, including cactus.
- At the Zoo they are offered seasonal fruit and vegetables, and a variety of freshly cut plant material.

RAINBOW LORIKEETS

What's for tea? Let me see
Someone's brought some fruit for me

That's not your fruit — that fruit's mine
Out of the way, you thieving swine!

Do your worst
I saw it first
You're out of line
This fruit is mine!

That's absurd
You silly bird
I saw this fruit
This fruit's my loot

Well — maybe we can make a deal
We'll seal a deal about this meal
It's almost more than I can bear
But how about . . .

All right, we'll share

DID YOU KNOW?

- Rainbow lorikeets are brightly coloured parrots found in the forests of Australia, Papua New Guinea, Indonesia, New Caledonia and the Solomon Islands.
- The rainbow lorikeet has a brush-tipped tongue. The tongue has tiny hairs on the end which soak up nectar from flowers and gather pollen from blossoms.
- In New Zealand, rainbow lorikeets should be kept in aviaries. They cannot be released into the wild because they might eat our native birds' food.

SUMATRAN TIGER

I'm usually not a messy eater
Like to leave my table neater
But really, what am I to do
With all these feathers?
What would you?

When you sit down to feast on chicken
Yummy, scrummy, whisker-lickin'
You'd think that folk would try at worst
To take the feathers off it first

But not for tigers
No such luck
Good thing I'm learning
How to pluck

Oh-oh — I think a sneeze is close
I've got a feather up my nose

DID YOU KNOW?

- This is Nisha, Auckland Zoo's only Sumatran tiger. She was born in Wellington Zoo in 1996 and came to Auckland in 1998.
- Tigers are predators, so they hunt other animals. They can also catch and eat fish.
- A tiger eats up to 45kg of meat in one meal. That's equivalent to a human eating 40 hamburgers in one go!
- At the Zoo, Nisha's meals are made more interesting by feeding her at different times, hiding her food or nailing it up on posts.

CALIFORNIAN SEALION

Here's a man
He's got a fish
Now can I catch it? Ooh I wish

To catch my fish
I'll have to sorta
Jump up high above the water

I'll flex my flippers
Just like so
Then kick my tail and up I go

Wheeeeeee!
Hold it lower, silly man
Now can I get it? Yes I can

Hey that was great
Hey that was fun
Perhaps he's got another one

I'll jump again
With any luck it
Might be there, inside his bucket

DID YOU KNOW?

- Senior Zoo keeper Andrew Coers is presenting a sealion demonstration with female Californian sealion Kipper.
- In the wild, sealions hunt for their food: fish, squid, octopus and crabs.
- Sealions are great divers and can hold their breath underwater for up to 15 minutes!

ASIAN ELEPHANT

It takes lots to feed an elephant
'Cause elephants need food
And not to feed an elephant
Is really rather rude

The elephant's by far the biggest
Creature in the Zoo
Not only is her body huge,
Her appetite is too

So if you have an elephant
Around one night for tea
Forgive her, if she eats a little
More than you and me

'Cause elephants need food, you see
They'll eat and eat until
That great big tummy's full, and that's
A lot of room to fill

DID YOU KNOW?

- Kashin (pictured) and Burma are the Zoo's two Asian elephants.
- Elephants are herbivores. They eat leaves, grasses, bark and roots.
- Elephants eat with their trunks, which are powerful enough to pull up young trees by the roots, but can just as easily curl around twigs and delicately snap them off.
- An elephant also uses its trunk to drink, but not as a straw! Instead, it sucks the water up into its trunk, and then squirts it into its mouth. Baby elephants need lots of practice to learn how to do this.

For Emma Rose — who helped to write this book

National Library of New Zealand Cataloguing-in-Publication Data

Gadsby, Jon.
The zoo. Feeding / by Auckland Zoo, Jon Gadsby.
ISBN 1-86941-753-4
1. Zoo animals—Juvenile literature. 2. Animals—Food—Juvenile
literature. (1. Zoo animals. 2. Animals—Food.) I. Auckland
Zoological Park. II. Title.
591.53—dc 22

A RANDOM HOUSE BOOK
Published by
Random House New Zealand
18 Poland Road, Glenfield, Auckland, New Zealand

First published 2005

Auckland Zoo logos and images © Auckland Zoological Park 2003
© 2005 photographs Auckland Zoo; text Random House

The moral rights of the authors have been asserted

ISBN 186941 753 4

Cover and text design: Sarah Elworthy
Auckland Zoo photography: Graham Meadows Ltd
www.gmpl.co.nz
Printed in China by Everbest Printing Co Ltd